Say Hello Koala

Photography Steve Parish
Words Pat Slater

Steve Parish
PUBLISHING

Koala
sleeps all day
in a tree.

At night
koala and possum
wake up.

K oalas
are
very good
at
climbing
trees.

Koala
reaches out
to grab
a tasty gumleaf.

Koala chooses
the very best
of all the leaves.

Mother koala
carries her baby.

Baby koala
watches mother
and learns to pick
the best leaves.

The kookaburra laughs loudly at the koala holding a leaf.

The koala hides
in the bush.

A tawny frogmouth
looks at koala
from big yellow eyes.

Koala is very happy to see a friendly possum.

A koala with dark fur watches a koala with light-coloured fur.

Koala sits
in the sun
and hears
butcherbird
singing.

Koala smells
the gum blossoms
and is very happy.

Say Goodbye

Koala

WITH THANKS
Ian Morris provided the photograph of the possum.